A

Journey

for

Better

Living

Just less

The

Baggage!

T- Marie Robertson

This book is dedicated to my family:

My mother, the late Minister Patricia Doughty, has taught me to believe in myself and go after whatever I want to achieve in life. She has taught me to smile regardless of any circumstance. She allowed my opinion to matter. I love you very dearly.

My husband, Don, how I admire you as a man, father and husband. You have never been selfish when I needed to write. You have encouraged me all the way. Thank you for your patience, love and understanding.

My son, DJ, has listened even when I know you didn't desire too, but believed in me all the way. Thank you.

My daughter, Dajah, has been my proof reader every time I write. I appreciate and thank you greatly.

My Granddaughter, Aubrey has been a precious bundle of joy.

Acknowledgements

I would like to first thank God, from whom all blessings flow. Thank You for giving me the desires of my heart.

My dad, Herbert Doughty, who also encouraged me to write poetry and was one of my listening ears. Thank you.

April Reaux, I thank you much. You are amazing.

I would like to acknowledge Missy, with Missy's Radio for putting me in touch with great contacts. Girl you really rock.

Cosha Hayes with Bran Nu Productions thanks for your time and patience.

To everyone that had a hand to lend at any given time. I thank you and appreciate you beyond measure.

To my nieces and nephews, that keeps me with a heart of laughter. Love you all.

To my God Mother, Jackie Vaughn has been a blessing to me, always keeping me in her prayers.

Itinerary of Content

Prologue

The reading and applying of this book is your ticket to a journey of a life time. It is all-inclusive. It helps too free the mind, feeds the spirit and helps to forgive in the heart by teaching you how to build on your faith, to self-motivate, display positive energy exchange, readying yourself when duty calls, confront hurts and learn when to hold on and or let go. We must learn to create our own paradise so that we can reside there daily. This trip also aids you in ridding yourself of baggage, diminishes burdens and release stress. This may be one of the only journeys that you can take much baggage as possible with you and not be offended if it is lost. So, change your mind, change your thinking, change your attitude and change your life as we journey on. Take notice I never mention it being easy but you must want a different outcome bad enough to withstand transformation.

Introduction

Have you ever been so consumed by the trials of life, feeling totally overwhelmed by day-to-day pressure of school, work, bills, health, spouse, motherhood, fatherhood, family, friends, matters of the heart, etcetera? Do you feel you just need a hug, a positive word, a reprieve or just a counsel of sorts, but there's not one tangible being available to console you? "It would be so much easier," we say, "if every time we need something or someone they're at our beckoning calls." Well, it's not design that way, which allows us to become stronger in our faith. Helping to create a more independent being. In other words, it helps us to grow up. This may seem hard sometimes and even unfair. We must know that mistakes teach a lesson, and preachers preach lessons, so it is imperative we obey God learn of Him to know how to live.

We need to view any problem we encounter as a learning experience because nothing happens by chance. Get as much knowledge as possible so that we can learn from it; use it for what it is worth and move on. Expect a gain from each encounter although sometimes the outcome may not be in your favor. We must exercise our minds because this is where all the information is stored and processes take course in our lives. Therefore, to have the mind of Christ in us, is best and to keep faith in God and never doubt.

Confronting situations and accepting positive criticism should not be frowned upon. We can experience a more paradise way of living but we must be willing to let go. This is a beneficial merit to self. We must initiate and change the process of our thinking and exercise what we want so when something we don't want comes to our mind we will not be receptive of it.

A blueprint is needed to build your dream house but faith is needed to start the designing of the blueprint. The bigger your faith the bigger the blueprint and foundation is laid accordingly. The handling of any situation is based upon the foundation and construction in which it was built. A good foundation can hold it together; therefore, don't build anything on quicksand. -A solid rock one shall remain. Come tour with me as it will help in helping you to become healed and spiritually whole.

Island of Faith

Here we will take an overdue vacation that can change your life over time. The only thing you will need for this trip is an open mind, willing spirit and a desire for change. This tour embarks upon the Island of Faith and disembarks at Paradise of Prosperity. This spiritual vacation destination can become a resident in your spirit. While journeying through the Island of Faith you may want to take notes, photos and so forth. Never let this memorable moment escape you. We will tour through faith building, faith scenarios, and first the meaning of faith.

Faith is defined by Dictionary.com as "Confidence or trust in a person or thing; belief that is not based on proof; belief in God or in the doctrines or teachings of religion. "So, we know that faith is placed in other people, things and or higher beings.

We all have some measure of faith noticed or unnoticed. We, as people tend to lose faith for different reasons, but it depends on the foundation in which our faith was initially built, will be the determining factor. We also may know faith to be "…the substance of things hoped for, the evidence of things not seen," Hebrews 11:1. (Belief not based on proof.) We all have been tried by faith to some degree. Faith is what you believe in, and if you believe, you will achieve.

When we were younger most of us believed in Santa Claus, Easter Bunny, Tooth Fairy and so on. We never saw them, but from our beliefs they would always leave gifts, candy or money. We tend to believe more when results or evidence appears. It is better to our understanding when it happens almost immediately.

I would like you to take this time to think back as far your mind will allow. Try to recall when you first learned to ride your bike, tie your shoelace, toss a ball, studied and passed a test. All of this was done by some form of faith; believing that you could do it. From the initial pedaling, the looping of the shoelace and the tossing of a ball, you did it without doubt. In all scenarios, your actions produced an affect but your mind adhered to your actions of what you really wanted, and that granted a positive result.

As employees, we believe that when we go to work, we will receive a paycheck for the work we're hired to do. If we didn't believe this, many of us would not go to work. What would be the reward?

Everything that we may believe is physical or tangible; from the toys Santa leaves to the pay check. We should place just a grain of that faith or belief in God. He is the giver of all rewards yet some doubt because they can't see a result with the naked eye immediately, although transformation may be taking place. We must learn to build on the faith that has no proof and as per Proverbs 3:5v says, "lean not to our own understanding." (NIV)

Isaiah 53:5 says, "…by His stripes we are healed." Some may not see that they are actually healed by Jesus 's stripes, but the truth is, we all are healed by His stripes to some degree. No one should put all their trust in your Dr. but you must get check- ups and follow Doctor's orders as well. Yes, faith in GOD is grand but faith without works is dead. Your action is getting regular check-up and if needed and to take the prescribed medications until you are totally healed from whatever sickness or disease that may be on you.

For those, who are dependents of their five senses only, miss out on healing and miracles because of their wavering faith. Learn to see with your spiritual eyes. Be steadfast and unmovable. If you are poor, think that you are rich; if you are sick know that you are healed and if you are broken know that you are whole by your faith and the will of God. You must obey God because faith without works is dead. Remember it's your belief that is housed in the mind so what you set in the mind is what you will obtain.

Stir up your Faith

Some people feel they have no faith or beliefs. What is not realized is a form of faith is activated every single day.

To keep faith is not always as easy as one may think. We may have had many trials and tribulations that sometime cause us to waver. Matthew 17:20 says, "If ye have faith as a grain of mustard seed, ye shall say unto this mountain, remove hence to yonder place; and it shall remove; and nothing shall be impossible unto you." Faith is also one's belief and the mustard seed is the smallest seed that can be planted. It does not take much belief in a higher being to move mountains (any problem or anything). We just must believe and not doubt because you will be without.

I Do!

I just married my faith; building on it and encouraging it daily, keeping a strong mate. We are together until death do us part; never to abandon it, keeping it close to my heart. To honor, love, cherish and obey. Forever shall my faith be with me. It is for better or worse, in sickness or health, poorer and wealth. ~Yes! I do. I will continue to stay true to my faith.

It is a good habit to place your -self in the company of people or a team that is wealthy in faith. They can help build you up when your faith is low. The team of faithfulness will coach you until you are strong enough to know and play your position like you were created to do. There really isn't an "I" in team, so I can't run this race alone. You know when your favorite baseball team is on the field and a good pitch is thrown? As the ball is twirling through the air, the opposing team's yelling, "Batter, batter, batter… Swing!" While your team yell's encouraging words to each other like, "You can do it! You can make it! "If God be for you, who can be against you!" By the time, they are finish your faith should be stable enough for your beliefs to conquer your hard time and build your faith and hit the ball out of the park or have the belief that it can be done.

I remember a couple of years back I was on a jobsite and I walk from my area to another area of this facility. As I was walking the paramedics hastily walked by me. I wasn't in no hurry. It wasn't unusual for them to be where I was so it really didn't alarm me. When I got closer to where they were. I notice some co-workers crying and moving about. So, I walk a little further to see a young lady lifelessly lying on the ground. The paramedics had called a code on her. Which means dead. Some was saying called the family. I walk to where they were. I started calling the young ladies name and Jesus over and over. Out of all the people this one fireman had walk up ask how old was the decease and as I remember someone saying, "She was in her thirties". I am still calling on Jesus, and calling out her name just fanning the air and calling on Jesus all at the same time over her all while this angel fireman saw fit that she was worth fighting for. When this particular fireman heard the age he again said, "No she is too young". I am still fanning and calling on Jesus like it was one of my sisters. By the time, he finished with his CPR and me with Jesus she had a pulse. All I could do is thank God, Thanking Jesus for saving grace and his healing powers. Thanking Him for a second chance.

I shared this to let you know that Jesus is real. My faith and the fireman works spun a reaction from God. To this day, she is alive and well. We should know who surrounds us, who knows what to do and who to call on when all else fails. My God! Know the company you keep. Know who will call out for you. My faith didn't fail me. I was happy that God was in the midst.

Great minds think alike. Wouldn't you like to be around like-minded people that could aid you back to good positioning and pray you back to your right stance? You should not want to be unequally yoked in any affair. We need people on our teams that care enough to give us a push or even hold our hand if we need it and vice versa. When we want to throw in the towel we better hope someone cares enough to pray us back to the place we belong and not have an 'I don't care if you don't care attitude.' We must choose our mates, friends and team players wisely.

Front Runners

No two mountains are identical; much like everyone's temperament.

We all handle mountains (problems) differently, not to say someone else can't help us with what is before us to handle today.

Note: The conquered trials of our fathers, mothers, sisters and/or brothers of yesterday are told today to aid in tomorrow's trials to come. In other words, what we may be going through today, someone else has been there and survived, and it is told in their testimonies/stories, which are to help us. We must learn what our importance is in this life and to know what our story or testament is.

I believe the lyrics to a song I recall that goes like this, "What don't kill us, will make us stronger," and it goes on to say, "Well I must be the world's strongest woman." The message is a testimony to let everyone know what she has been through and survived; that she never gave up. We should keep the faith and never doubt too. We are much stronger than we imagine but we sometimes become complacent in the state that we are in. Do not get confused with knowing how to be abased, abound or content in the state that you are in.

I find that we give the devil too much credit when things appear to not be in our favor immediately. Don't become impatient. I would merit that to the new age of 'having it like yesterday' and sometimes becoming lackadaisical, or to say it plainly, just lazy. We may settle for what has been offered on the first run; wanting everything to be given instead of working for it. We may sometimes fight for the wrong causes, but remember choosing our battles is up to us. We tend to choose what is easiest to obtain or what takes less energy. When there is so much more for us, but lack of actions causes lack of blessings. Just remember that every choice has a consequence.

Everything has become so 'microwaved,' from earning degree online to home-based businesses, socializing, banking and so forth. One almost never should leave the comfort of their homes for anything. We need to be more appreciative of the simplicity today's technology has afforded us. We are so unlike our grandmothers and grandfathers, who while in their hardest of times, were praying for the things we have now and some of us take it all for granted. Their faith was not an immediate result but they believed and never doubted. Let's thank them by living up to our full potential. Let their legacies live on by becoming all that we can be, lawyers, doctors, authors, teachers, nurses, entrepreneurs, social workers, policeman, fireman and so on. Just give it all you have. We lose by not trying, we win when we give it our all.

Testimonies

In hopes of enabling someone to gain faith or renew their faith, I will share my testimonies of faith-filled events that have occurred in my life, where I never gave up the faith or belief. Perhaps just to give insight on faith and how faith seeds are also real.

I will start with the passage of James 2:20, "But wilt thou know, O foolish man, that faith without works is dead?"

1. In the summer of 1990 in New Orleans, my husband had stated to me that we needed a loaf of bread. I said, "Okay," knowing I didn't have a penny. I drove to the supermarket on a bright, sunny day. I park my car, closed my eyes, let out a sigh, removed the keys from the ignition and proceeded onto the store, I had been praying the entire time to myself. "Lord I need to get a loaf of bread."

I remember the wind just started blowing out of nowhere. Now, remember this was summer in the South. I knew something was manifesting, because it just felt different. The wind was blowing towards me. It was hard enough that the small objects on the ground was lifted and moving about. I was focused on my thoughts, while watching everything flowing around me. As the wind ceased right before me, there was a piece of paper or so I thought. I stoop to pick it up and burst into laughter it was a $5 bill. It was just what I needed and more. As you may note I never had one doubt or unbelief. I said, "Thank you Lord." He had done it again for me. That's worth a praise and more. Major to me. He may not come when you want him, but he is always on time.

2. I was living in apartments near Read Boulevard in New Orleans in the spring of 1992, with no money in the bank or in my pockets, to say the least. I was on my way to work but had no money for transportation to get me there. I was young and prideful, left my apartment with one thing on my mind… catching the public transit. I think at that time it cost $1.25 for the fare, however praying and walking out of my apartment gates, I turned to the right, which was another apartment complex. As I walked along the pavement approximately 40 steps away from the bus stop, there lay two balled-up $1.00 bills. Yes, tithes and offering has much to do with this which also will be explained later. There wasn't a moment where I doubted. I simply kept the faith.

Neither of those times did I cry or complain. It was simply time for action. Remember the scripture, "Faith without works is dead." During those events, it was no time for a funeral or a pity party; action was required. I needed a monetary blessing and I received it because I never doubted and I acted on what I believed.

Money may not be the thing you're asking for now, however, pray, believe and receive; whether it's praying for peace of mind, a new car, house, bills to be paid, patience, anxiousness, health, strength, transformation, a job, or even standing in the gap for someone else. Just bring it to God and leave it there. Be patient and don't doubt because you will be without.

This was only two of the many times my faith has kept me and me keeping the faith. My actions spun a reaction from God. Sometimes we might sit and complain about what we don't have and/or the process of obtaining it, but we should move on what we know being the word and what we sow, which is our planting/giving.

Giving comes in all forms; from church offerings and tithes, to giving to other people in need, organizations, schools and etcetera. Giving is not always monetary. It could be your time, clothes, shoes, cars, your expertise anything that would be a benefit to another person or organization. Keep that faith and build on it always. Do know that when you are faced with a problem that is too hard for you, it would be a benefit to help others with their problem and watch how GOD moves on your behalf. What I am saying is take the focus off you, GOD knows your needs and help others and GOD will help you because of your unselfishness.

Faith is like a flower.

You must water it every day.

Will it grow and prosper

Or

will you let it wither away?

Faith also comes by hearing.

What word have you heard today?

Is it a word you should hold on too?

Or one you should let slip away.

Faith without works is dead

And

We are much a live, never should we part from it,

Until we are on the other side.

Faith building is a process and we should learn to build on our faith each day, but we must know we can't have faith today and disbelief tomorrow. It will not add up. We can start by becoming more mindful when using or activating our beliefs.

Let's take a quick moment, if you are sitting then stand up and walk three to four feet away from the place you are sitting. Return to the place and sit gently in the same place. Did you feel that faith was activated or this is something you have always taken for granted? Faith requires actions and we act before we sat, which initiated a response. The sit held you up.

Think about this as well. Can you go through a closed door that isn't automatic or do you just stand there until it magically opens for you? Nothing will take place until you take your hand place it on the handle and turn or push it open. Complaining will not open it nor will crying. You may be delayed if you are waiting on someone else to do it for you. It requires actions your actions to get it done. You must also believe and not doubt, but know when you just believe and not doubt without the actions the door will still be closed unto you. Apply this rule to initiate faith, B.A.P. you must believe, act and pray. Anything in life that you want, action is required by you to obtain whatever it is. You can achieve whatever your mind has conceived but action, determination and maybe a few sacrifices are required. Trust God, he can and he will work in your behalf. you must believe in him and not doubt. This can't be stressed enough.

Hunting Desires

Animals learn from a young age, to eat one must hunt. So, anything you desire you must go after it. We are the hunter of our success, happiness and dreams. Blaming others for what we are lacking is an excuse on the account of self. Something as simple as when we get out of the shower we are naked until we decide to put clothes on, therefore, we are not educated until we decide to learn, we are broke until we decide to work and save, we are burdened until we yet decide to let it go, we are obese until we decide to eat healthy and exercise and so forth; it is just what it is.

We are what we are and we have what we have until we decide we have faith and do the work. Take your complaining and turn it into an action tool for every complaint you have replace with an action for the betterment of your situation.

Stop dying of thirst in a pool of pure water. Also, let nothing or no one distract you; just as Peter did when Jesus called out to him from the boat. He could walk on the water until he took his eyes off Jesus. Keep the faith and never doubt let your visions be your goal leaving distractions out. We tend to accomplish more when we are focus on the goal at hand major or minor. I know before I go to sleep at night I give a quick mental note to self of what I would like to take on the next day and complete. My subconscious reminds me the next waking morning of what I am set out to fore fill, therefore my actions become receptive of my request and my will see it through. It may not always happen just as planned but keep exercising the right of passage until you are comfortable where you are. Yes, some people is deemed to stay in place longer than others and that is sometimes do to us not learning the lesson at hand that is being taught. In school one can't matriculate until lessons are learned and proven.

Identifying Faith

Before we move on to the next port, identify some things you may have thought that just 'happened' or you figured it was just luck. It is better to give credit to God for His blessings, as opposed to chalking it up to 'just luck.'

We should make a faith journal and a list of how faith has taught us and brought us through many trials and hardships. Also, list how your faith has progressed. Then go back to the journal as a reminder when things seemed hard; realize what got you through those experiences although the matter may differ, however faith is the basis to it all.

God never changes; circumstances do. Allow your list to bring back to your remembrance of times when your faith in God sustained you. Remember faith without works is dead. We waste time if we complain and complaining doesn't help the situation it hinders it.

The next time you take a seat know that your faith has been activated to know that the seat will hold you. Have enough faith to know that trusting in God, He would console you.

Reaching the port

We have just toured the beautiful Island of Faith. There is no other like it. It is individualized by its maker. Place the date when you first visited here. Live by it forever. Let the building of your faith be your souvenir. As a favorite woman, I know once said, "Don't bend, don't bow and Don't break." Keep the faith.

Faith Always Includes Trusting Him

Chapter II

Self-Motivation Mountains

As we climb the Mountains of Self–Motivation, taking on the altitude of its peak we may only need to adjust our attitudes. It is up to us how high we can climb and how long we soar. This chapter will teach how motivation and faith tie-in together. We will be able to identify or distinguish how on the Island of Faith you can see the mountain peaks of self-motivation.

Self-motivation, as defined by Dictionary.com is "initiative to undertake or continue a task or activity without another's prodding or supervision." Self-starter comes to mind also, which is one who initiates a project or work without being told to do so. When we know, a task needs to be done, we just do it- good work ethics. However, for some, they can be the best employee, friend, spouse or advisor but when it comes to themselves, they lean on others instead of taking the advice they give to others.

There are times when there's no tangible being to talk too in times of need; making some to feel sad, lonely, neglected or depressed. This seems unfair because they make themselves available for others to lean on in tough times.

We had never stop to think especially in our moments that we need to sort through what God allowed before us, but what we must know is that if GOD allowed it before us and HE is the creator of it all He will see us through it.

We must marry our beliefs and know without out a shadow of doubt that we can accomplish whatever we set our minds to do it shall be done. Know that our faith should stand through sickness, health, rich, poor, the good and the bad. We must have continuous belief even when the odds are stacked against us. We need to be totally for it because to be against it, we fail.

So, get it right and stay right! Also, it's good to get yourself right before rendering yourself or pairing with another person, but this topic along may have to be told in its own book; we will leave that for later.
Yes, we sometimes become compromised for various reasons but we must stay true to our beliefs. Our beliefs should motivate us to know we can do whatever it takes without doubt to get a task done.

Faith with Works

Self-motivation and faith should be a combination. Having faith without motivation of self is like having a car with no keys. It just won't start.

I sometimes refer to a story of "The Little Engine that Could." When the little engine saw a humongous mountain to climb, doubt immediately set upon him. I can only imagine his thought process. "I may tire out. It may take too long. I may fall back down. I can't do this alone. I don't have enough energy. I won't ever make it up there, and if I get up there, what's next, etcetera, etcetera, etcetera." Giving every negative thought of doubt as to why he doesn't deserve what he has the right too. The top of the mountain.

Good thing his mind didn't believe what his eyes were telling it to believe. So, he decided to go with his mind and then spoke, "I think I can." "I think I can." (Oh, I can feel a praise coming and no longer the thought of *I can't*.) This immediately stirred up his faith and motivated him into action. Again, he repeated, "I think I can."

He started his engine and started slowly up the mountain. He continuously chanted in pep rally form along the way, "I think I can. I think I can. I think I can… He put behind him what is his mother said, "he can't do it", what the teacher said, "he will never learn", what his Father said, "your too small", "Before long he was on top of the mountain. He placed all odds behind him. He was then able to look out to the Island of Faith and view how it had increased to put him in the place he stood chugging and prancing around. (I now feel a dance coming on.) His problem is now being beneath him.

Nobody was there to tell him what should be done, and the mountain did not come with instructions stating how to reach the top of it. We must take the initiative to get the job done. We must motivate ourselves to read the word of God, which would be a benefit to us. To call back to God his promises to us. Faith stirred up the engine's motivations, which activated his will and he was willing to climb the mountain. All this action was taken place in the mind first, which led to him accomplishing his goal.

(Yes, all of this from a cartoon.) Can you feel something changing even with your own situation? This is good reason to keep the mind healthy and free of clutter to not allow hindrance of thoughts.

Don't worry anymore, with prayers and belief that it could be done than God moves. Speak it, believe it and receive it. Like the Little Engine, mountains may be in our paths, but have faith to move them out the way. Some mountains, we will need to fast, pray and do as God commands us to move them or obscure them to the point there not so bothersome. Know that after it's moved, you will have a testimony that can help others move mountains that are in their lives.

Pep Rallies

Motivating yourself is an attribute that can be acquired by rehearsing and exercising or keeping the thought if I don't do it for me, then who will. We won't always have someone physically cheering us on. This is not to hurt us, but to help us be more independent and mature being.

Sports games are likely to be won because of their practicing, their talent and the motivational chants, pep rallies and speeches they hear and believe.

We must give ourselves pep talks and rallies of our own before we can face our problems. I will only name a few and you can place whatever or whoever it is with this, A job interview, test results, old habits, new job, going back to school, raising children, being a spouse, going to court, illnesses, addictions other people and finally sometimes self. It doesn't matter what the mountain is. This is for the one that just said, I did this before well do it again be assertive and don't doubt. Go to the higher being and talk to them if it is the will it will be so. Remember you want be promoted until all lesson are learned successfully. So, past the test the first time the lesson is taught so we can move on.

Let's take the late great Mohammad Ali, he did not win all his fights because of his techniques and skills alone. It was his beliefs and self-motivational speeches to himself and to the world he repeated often as chants in pep rally form, "I am the greatest. Nobody can beat me. I am Mohamed Ali." It was set in his mind he believed and then did the work to achieve his goals. Remember you do not get the desire look from one exercise routine. Even talented people that could sing will not obtain a dynamic voice from one note held. It is the rehearsal the repetitive exercise of the vocals that get the desire ranges, keys and harmony.

How much more can we achieve with God, His Spirit and

Jesus in the equation? Let's take the story of David and Goliath, now. Because of David's faith and trust in God, he believed with no doubt that he would destroy Goliath. I am certain he called out Philippians 4:13 verse "I can do all things through Christ that strengthens me." His strength endured until the end. No matter the size of the circumstance with faith, prayers and Gods power anything can be devour.

Repeat this chant until it is embedded in your spirit or when you know that there is a change in you.

Motivate yourself.

Activate your mind.

Not just today but all the time.

Motivate yourself.

Activate your mind.

Not just today but all the time.

When you don't do for yourself what thy art too, why become upset when someone else doesn't do it for you?

Just Do It!

It is helpful to revert to the smallest of things as catchphrases like "I think I can" or "Just DO it," to motivate us to achieve. "I think I can" has helped me countless of times. Now, "Just DO it," is simple and inspires us to action; to do the work. Quit talking about it and just hush-up and do it! I love this catchphrase because of its simplicity and it works. You should get it done and just looking and staring, wondering and wishing will not get it done. It takes actions. If you say all day I am hungry and never stop to eat you will still be hungry until you fix it or get you something to eat you will still be hungry. Just do what needs to be done to get you full or nourished.

If someone says, "I will pass my test," but doesn't study for it and fails; how can he blame God or the teacher for something you did not prepare for? Let's remember, faith without works is dead. So, don't blame God for your lights or phone getting turned off when you had the money to pay the bill but spent it on nonsense. Do right with little things and He will grant you much. This is one of the reasons why some of us are not prosperous because we can't be trusted.

How to eat an elephant? One bite at a time of course. So, remind yourself to start small when accomplishing big things; do not focus on the size of a mountain to climb, just reach the top of it one step at a time. (With every step, you're one step closer to the top.) Doesn't it feel good when you accomplish a task, no matter how big or small, to then go and stamp it with "COMPLETED," not defeated? You know the task needs to be done, just start by picking up one thing at a time. Tell yourself, "I can do it," believe it and then start doing it. Before you realize it, it's completed and on to the next task. (When it comes to cleaning my kids' rooms, for example, this simple duty can be a major task.)

On the opposite note, if it is a habit or an addiction you are trying to get rid of, remove or reduce it in small increments until it's all gone or just stop it all at once (go cold turkey) per how much faith you have. Get professional help if needed and call on the elders of the church, which is great for support and counseling. Never be afraid or prideful to seek help from others. You may be surprised by the results of how outside help can aid you. Others advice, knowledge and expertise can lead to better results. Ask God to put people in your life that are good for your recovery and life change. Also, ask Him for the gift of discernment so that if the devil tries to send his people to lead you down another wrong path, you will know them by their fruits. Let us not dress a spoiled apple in an orange suit because it is your circumstance. It is what it is not because of whose it is.

Tell yourself I can get through this because with God all things are possible, (Matthew 19:26), and believe it. Write notes and place them where they can be seen and read daily; implanting them in your mind, guided in the Spirit. Watch things come to fruition as you speak with your mouth what is to happen in your life. Then believe what you have spoken and receive them according to God 's will for you.

Monkey on My Back

I used to be a shopaholic; shopping six days a week. The habit wasn't formed in an instance, and in my case, it didn't end in an instance. The shopping ventures continued for a period but I noticed I was going less each week because of my willingness to quit. During the process of quitting, I learned to analyze myself by taking mental notes of my daily routines, asking myself,

why am I in the mall shopping today?

What positive activity can I do to replace what I am doing right now?

I could put my money to better use.

I could be spending quality time with my family doing something together that everybody loves.

I can do this; I don't need to be here.

It is okay to reason with yourself. I have learned not to give an excuse to keep a habit. I have since become a healthier being with less baggage, literally, while living a healthier lifestyle. So, let go and let God's will be done in your life. If it takes using every fiber of your being to obey God, then so be it. It's well worth it!

I have found that time frames of developing habits differ from person to person, depending if one has an addicting spirit/personality, and the time frames for getting rid of habits differ as well. Like with any problem, addiction or habit, I first had to admit I had a problem. Second, I had to have the desire to change; want change. Next, I had to initiate the change; move into action and be a doer. Remember good change may not seem easy but it's easier than dealing with the outcome of keeping the bad habit. Getting a strong and healthy support group is a good benefit as well to saving your life and your soul from the pits of hell eternally. There is no earthly problem that should keep you addicted that heaven can't heal. Pray and ask to be loosed in the name of JESUS believe and not doubt.

Mind Changing!

Since our mind controls everything we do, it is better to have the mind of Christ in our body. That way when we pull thoughts to do anything big or small, it will be done right. "Let this mind be in you, which was also in Christ Jesus, "Philippians 2:5. Yes, change does start in the mind. Change of mind, changes habits. Know that other problems can stem from just one bad habit. People have lost families, jobs, homes and their lives because of bad habits or addictions. You must stay motivated by our will.

I remember when I first noticed how much I was shopping and spending, so I began to pray. I didn't fully turn everything over to God, out of fear He would take it all from me all together. So, I prayed half-heartedly but learned I still needed rescuing. The problem was still there. I had to decide to either let God handle the situation or try to work it out myself, which the latter didn't work for me. I found out, I had to trust God to take care of the situation entirely. It was all or nothing. Do not put any of it on reserve.

I have since learned how to manage shopping, and discovered that my excessive shopping habit was an escape from having to deal with a deeper problem. In other words, the shopping habit was only a cover-up to keep from dealing with another problem. After releasing the shopping addiction to God, the other problem was revealed and eventually got resolved. So, shopping was a habit that stemmed from the unresolved issue. I also learned there is cause and effect, and I no longer feel that I need to shop excessively because I no longer have the cause as an issue. It was a struggle for me at one time but has become manageable. I became motivated and wanted a change for the better. I needed to deal with my issues to make a better living for me, and it has.

Running

Running from a hill

can make you run into a mountain.

What is it that causes you to take flight?

What are you running from?

Stop running and get the problem solved.

Bring it to God.

You have problems?

The bible has solutions.

Deal with the matter before the matter deals with you.

How about You?

What are some of your habits? What are you addicted to? What do you feel you can't live without? What are your vices? Well, no matter how big, small, ugly or maybe cute, as some may call their habits, addictions, idols or vices, Jesus can replace them with things that are better for us, healthier for us; things that are more profitable for us; things that are more fun than we could even imagine for us. -True happiness, True joy, True love and True living. Enter the door of light, that door is Jesus. Yes, for you overeating is habitual and sometime it's replacing unresolved matters too.

Ask yourself:

Is my habit worth losing my family over?

Is it destroying the quality of life for my family?

Does it take me away from spending time with

people that truly matter?

Is it worth losing the things I have earned?

Is it worth having my name blotted out of the

Book of Life?

Is the hurt of yesterday and un-forgiveness worth holding onto and keeping me in bondage?

One of the first steps we take in getting our life back or obtaining a better life is to be willing admit the problem and having the ability of letting it go. Your addiction doesn't have a hold on you; it's you holding on to it. Release it. Let it go. When it calls your name, you call Jesus' name. "Give your burdens to the Lord," Psalm 55:22. Feel those burdens being lifted like a dove ascends into the sky.

Ask God to fill your life with things He wants you to do, and to fill your life with people He wants you to associate with.

Be patient in receiving what you pray to receive, however due expect it.

Substitutions

Bad habits or addictions oftentimes are cover-ups to a deeper problem or problems, whether they are formed to avoid feelings of neglect, hurt or some other pain or problem that exists. Some people may turn to substances, things and/or people that are unhealthy for them to depend on, in hopes of escaping a reality or trying to fill a void that exists in their lives. - Substituting reality for fantasy. Wherever it stems from remember they can be resolved.

Resorting to bad habits or addictions only compounds the problem. They do not solve the problem; they mask it. Regardless of what the problem is, turn to God and depend on Him, His Spirit and His son, Jesus. We are not alone on this earth. There are saints in heaven watching us and cheering us on to do right (Hebrews 12:1). Go to Jesus for patience, endurance, wisdom, understanding, love, joy and peace in solving every problem. Self-medicating with bad habits and/or addictions worsens the problem. Do you know more than Jesus?

Reminiscing!

I remember when I was young I would go to my mother for counsel or just to talk, but avoid going for a pity party. Her answers were straight to the point. If you didn't 't know her, you may have thought she was just cold, but it was just that she explained things in such a simple way.

For instance, I would go to her and say, "You know Mom, when I do this… This is what happens…, and it really hurts."

Her reply would be, "Did you like the hurt child?"

"No."

"Well don't do it again." Or "mom you know Sister Sue at church didn't speak to me."

Her reply would be, "Did you speak? Do your part and don't worry about anyone else."

Her answers were plain and simple.

Yes, this may be true, but what about the fight and the struggle, I would think, *it is just not that easy all the time.*

She never said it would be easy. I had to learn, we have choices of what we want in our lives. We are the drivers of our own lives. Pressing to make the mark we set for ourselves is only as important as we make it. No one can experience our entire life. With that said, if there's a habit or addiction you want out of your life, whether it's gambling, drinking, prostituting, smoking, experiencing with illicit drugs, stealing, cursing, fornicating, committing adultery, bisexuality, lying, manipulation or homosexuality, being abusive or whatever spirit has taken residence in your body, make the decision to evict it. Fast and pray as God's Spirit leads you to move it. Call on the elders of the church to agree that it has to go, because it is written in Matthews 18:19, "That if two of you shall agree on earth as touching anything that they shall ask, it shall be done for them of my Father which is in heaven. "

So, be steadfast; adamant, determined that the devil's spirit is not to dwell in your body. Do not allow anyone to reside in your body that doesn't have the power to pay anything for you. Jesus paid the price for your sins when He died on the cross and with Him we win but you must allow him to reside within you. Speak with power and authority, "Be thou removed from my body Satan, and be cast into the sea in the name, Jesus!" Do not have any doubt or unbelief in your heart. Believe you are saved from the spirit that wants to reside in your body. Be delivered out of bondage and be made free in Christ. Now, the transformation may feel like thirst in the desert, but be patient and endure. Stay motivated.

This is where your new life begins; a life of freedom. However, make certain that once the bad spirit is gone, do not allow it back, because its stronger the second time around. So, don't linger around where you know it is. Separate yourself from its dwellings. Come from among them.

Giant

There's a giant I want to slay today

and

I am motivated by my will,

but

if I see him with my naked eye.

He stands nearly ten feet high,

but

When I close my eyes

and

see him with my heart

I know I can tear it apart.

That giant isn't so big now,

because my faith, prayer and my will have torn him down.

Big, small, wide or tall,

I have the courage for them all.

Look at me now,

I am free.

I now have liberty.

This poem was written with all problems, mountains, habits and addictions in mind. I hope that you use these words of inspiration. I pray this will help you to tear down anything that stands in your way of obtaining your dreams, goals, accomplishments or anything that may be a hindrance to you.

When I wrote this poem, my daughter read it and she immediately said to me, "Oh mom I can use this to help me when it's thundering and lightening, so I won't be afraid anymore." Since hurricane Katrina, she had been absolutely terrified of thunder and lightning. She would cry in terror, running into our room at night to sleep with us if there was thunder and lightning. After I heard her reciting the poem to herself as it was thundering one day, she came running and screaming, but this time it was excitement and joy, not fear.

"Mom I did it! I didn't cry and I wasn't afraid."

She no longer runs into our room, crying hysterically, which is a blessing, and my hope is that the words help you or someone you know over -come whatever they are going through. Rehearse it a few times or make up your own chant to build your courage and faith.

Faith motivates courage and courage wards of fear. Think like David thought before he defeated Goliath. -Believe, speak it and do the work.

Size isn't everything!

Sometimes we look at people and situations according to size. Looks are sometimes deceptive to the naked eye. The size of the matter does not always consist of its power. Scorpions are small but they are mightier than a beast. They have been known to put people out with just one hit. Which would you prefer being small and mighty or large with no power?

So, faith with works moves mountains. Apply it to daily living. I was always told once we know better we must do better. We may not get every lesson on the first journey but stay the course. Motivate yourself to stay focus and do the best that you could do.

Pass it on!

As you may know, every lesson you learn isn't always just for you to hold on to. Share it. This is what knowledge is about, taking what we know and passing it on for the betterment of others. Teachers do it all the time. Every journey we take, we bring photos back to share the experience. Share this knowledge and its beauty. No vacation spot makes you a resident however allow motivation to reside in you. Pass it on.

Chapter III

The Gardens of Energy

This journey is to discover the energy field that surrounds us. What energy do we send into the atmosphere? What energy is returned to us? What fuels us? How do we change the atmosphere that surrounds us?

In this garden, we will learn that what we sow is what will grow. Come with me as we walk through the beautiful garden of energy. If need be, stop and smell the flowers, prune the weeds or uproot what isn't a need. Water the soil and wait for the harvest taking in the beauty that lies before us.

May I take your Order?

I have had the joy of reading various books by different authors, and observed that most authors are aware of the importance, words have in the world. What we send out verbally is what will come back to us. For instance, when a waiter asks, "What would you like to order?" Your answer goes out and you expect to receive it when it's ready. When we speak, think of it as you placing an order. If you order a T-bone, then that is what you expect to receive. When your daily order arrives don't be surprised to receive what your mouth requested. For example, someone speaks, "I will have a handsome man." Well, they receive a handsome man but he is rotten to the core. Specify what you want. If you want a T-bone medium rare, order just that, and if it is not what you ordered you do not have to accept it although you may have to deal with what has been requested. If you want a beautiful, Godly woman, then make your request known, (Philippians 4:6).

Let's go deeper. Remember in the book of Genesis when God said, "Let there be light," (Genesis 1:3)? That was declared with spoken words. This is in the first book of the bible to let us know the importance of words and that we can speak anything into existence because we are made in His image, (Genesis 1:27).

Science teaches us that both positive and negative energy exists in relation to ions, electrons, protons and such. Well, positive and negative energy also exists in the lives of people. We must know and understand which energy we put into the world because it is the exact same energy that will come back to us like a boom- a- rang. In other words, we get back from the atmosphere what we send out, just as, we can only withdraw from the bank what we deposit along with the interest earned.

We reap what we sow, (Galatians 6:7). Everything we speak and do returns to us. So, why speak derogatively to our children, spouses, neighbors, and so on. Do you not love yourself? Because if you do, there is no way you would mistreat someone else, knowing that it will come back to you.

Also, it is important to keep in mind, when someone asks, "How are you doing?" Don't answer, "I feel bad, I am broke, frustrated, sick, or what have you, sometimes that's your emotions and not you. "Reply with positive words, if that's what you want in your life. You have the power of life and death in your tongue, (Proverbs 18:22).

Some may say repetitive degrading name calling of any kind is not offensive and should not cause low self -esteem. I beg to differ. We were taught the color of red in preschool/kindergarten by repetition and when we see it our mind immediately know that it is red. If we are constantly called stupid, ugly, fat, dumb, and other names I refuse to mention we begin to subconsciously see ourselves in that manner. This is very negative and is a form of abuse and should not be tolerated by any means.

Mental note: Most outbursts evoke the most negative response and if this is true let us try answering slower to think of the response. Repeat the response inwardly than let it expel. Do whatever skill that you can come up with to say what you actual mean. When encounter in a negative manner or a negative response ensues remember this acronym A P.R.A.Y.E.R.

A Positive Reaction Allows Your Exuberant Response!

Changing your Energy

Let's imagine you have two containers that are the same size. Take all the hurt you have been holding on to like pain, fear, jealousy, anger, bitterness, grief, neglect, stress, low self-esteem abuse etcetera and put them all into one of the containers. Now, it may be full, half full, partially full or may be even empty if you are a pure and perfect person. We will name this container L.I.G.

Next, take the other empty container and fill it with things you have asked God for but may have never received. This container will be named H.O.T. Now take the H.O.T. container and pour as much of it as possible into the L.I.G. container without letting it overflow. I guess you are asking what the purpose of this is. Well, it's to get you to see how or why we may miss our blessings.

There may be too much junk blocking the way for God's blessings to come in. Kick the devil's spirit out, which is the spirit that is out to destroy you and others, and receive the Spirit of God, which is the spirit that is out to save you and others from all those things that kill, steal or destroy. Spirits need a body and it's up to us to decide which we want residing in our body. Who do you want to rent too? Remember Jesus has already paid the price and with the devil you will be paying the price,

As you may have notice the L.I.G. you should let it go and the H.O.T. you should hold on too so we can have in us all that GOD has for us.

Restoration!

We sometimes tend to become hoarders of mental clutter to some degree. This is deformation to a healthy spirit. We are not hopeless, yes this can be help but we must decipher what and why we allow the overload of a tainted vessel.

Even computers know when there is too much of the wrong stuff stored. They start to run differently, slower, freezes up and sometimes worse, they may crash. However, for computers they come from the manufacturer with a restoration disc to rectify. We need to know when things are not right in us. Go back to our manufacturer, God, who will have His son, Jesus cleanse us of all filthiness. He already knows what needs to be removed before we ask. He's just waiting on us to make the decision to let them go, since we have free will.

Negativity!

Negative energy tries to break you down but positive energy lifts you. Negativity can come from what we allow others to dump on us like gossiping. This reminds me of a poem that I had written years past. Plant this seed in your garden water and nurture it, watching it grow.

I am not a trash can.
Don't dump your trash on me.
Whether you realize it or not it could leave stains and odors you
see.
I could lend you my ear or even give sound advice
but
Dropping unwanted trash isn't always nice.
My can has a lid you need permission to open it up.
Too much unwanted trash can make any one stinky or corrupt.
You will get a fine if you liter and talk is not always cheap.
So be mindful of how you handle your trash, burn it up and set it
free.
Watch out for those litter bugs that's always throwing garbage
around the town.
You are accepting their trash today
But tomorrow they will be throwing your trash on the ground.
Let's clean up our lives and our city,
Because
litter is just not pretty.

In essence let's not be so eager to except from anybody, something about somebody that could cause a mishap with everybody because of nobody.

Also, negativity may come from walking in the shadow of bad childhood experiences. The devil will try and enter anyway he thinks he can to leave you with no energy, ill or even worse.

Don't water negativity,

Because it is sure to grow.

Making you frown and weighing you down.

Let positive energy flow.

Snipping off the limbs will only prune the tree.

Uproot it and set it free.

Speaking your wants into existence,

Just lose the negativity.

Gossip!

Gossip is defined as idle talk or rumor about the personal or private affairs of others. When we talk about the personal affairs of others, keep in mind how we would want someone else to converse about our affairs. It is okay to say to people you don't care to hear gossip. If they are bold enough to spread gossip, we can be bold enough to say we don't want to hear it, but if you do discuss others private life, don't do it to make yourself look good. Strength is not gained at the expense of others.

Some people gossip because they don't want to feel alone in the rut they are in. Negative people feed on drama, whether it is from television, news, text messages, hair shops, newspapers, church house and etcetera. We all have had someone gossip about us and know that the gossip can simply be a lie. Some people want objects to be cursed, but negativity is spread by people via objects. In other words, objects are the vehicle for negativity, but people are the drivers.

Where do You Fill Up?

Certain grades and brand of gas may make some vehicles run differently. Per your cars manual will have which grade of gas to purchase. When I am in a hurry I might get gas at Mr. Off Brand gas station instead of my normal routine gas station, only to notice later that my car runs sluggish or starts knocking making unfamiliar sounds. However, when I get my gas routinely at Mr. Brand name gas station, where I normally fuel up on the regular basis, my car rides fine. No sluggishness, knocking the acceleration is great and I can get more mileage.

The moral of this story is when we are feeling low or in a state of being naïve, we definitely should not stop just anywhere to refuel because you don't want to make a bad situation worse. Don't be susceptible to things that are bad for you, even in your most vulnerable state. We care about what fuels our vehicle; how much more should we care what fuels us? We wouldn't put a banana in our gas tank, so how much more is it important to put the right things into our bodies. Stop breaking your routine and get what you know makes you run faster, longer and better.

People tend to make bad decisions when they are in a vulnerable state. Here's an example:

People tend to make poor decisions when they are hungry. Have you heard the saying, "It's not good to grocery shop when you're hungry?" Well, it's true. People tend to chuck food into their baskets, which eventually goes straight to their hips and belly, in which they wouldn't normally choose. Choosing sugary foods leads to abnormal blood sugar spikes and sluggish feeling a few hours later. We all should be careful about food choices this not just for diabetics. Also, they may eat more when they're very hungry. Sticking to a more organized and healthy routine would minimize this greatly. Well, the same behavior can be found when people long to be in a relationship, have a job, or some other activity. Don 't be desperate and accept anything. "Be anxious for nothing" Philippians 4:6. You're worth more than that. Making hasty choices can be detrimental in relationships, business decision and much more. A quick fix can cause one to needing longer healing process.

King of the Jungle!

Lions and tigers are born destroyers of the wild, but they too are eaten when they are at their weakest. You are always being watched believe it or not. They have people that sits and prey upon others. Therefore, we should always pray and put on the whole armor of God so if the person who preys tries to attack, the person who prays and keeps God's commandments will be protected.

So, tap into your energy and reach into the atmosphere far and beyond any mountain that may have once stood in your way. Remember the smallest bit of positive is still more than any amount of negative. Make great decisions no matter what state of mind you are in. It will pay off in the long run. Have integrity. Stand your ground. Think of Shadrach, Meshach and Abednego. They stood their ground no matter the circumstance.

Positivity

Passion drives a change

Of heart that starts in the mind, this

Sometimes help you to be so kind.

In engaging thoughts

to be a better me. Wash me with Your blood Jesus; remove my

Iniquities, because this is where I find

Victory.

In trusting God, He

transformed my life.

You can change too, getting rid of all negativity and strife.

Names, Titles and Labels

Everything has a name, title or label. This is how we refer to things, people, animals, and etcetera. If a child is constantly called something they are not, it is very likely they will start to believe they are what they are being called. For instance, if a child is constantly told they are just like their father who is a jailbird, then they may believe they are just like their father, a jailbird. Their behavior and actions will line right up with what a jailbird is. If you don't want your child to be stupid, then don't call him or her stupid. Words are very important. Remember God made the entire earth by speaking it into existence. You want your child to grow up being productive, successful, healthy, joyous, peaceful, loving…all the things that are of God? Then, call children those titles, names or labels. Keep in mind, children do grow up and they remember if they were mistreated or if they had a great childhood.

We need to lead by example. Don't be a do as I say parent and not as you see. This has a tendency of confusing children. If you don't want your child to be in an abusive relationship when they get older, then don't allow yourself to be in an abusive relationship. If you don't want your kids to smoke, drink, or curse, then don't do it around them. This is not to say they want learn these behaviors elsewhere. Make it unfamiliar to them. Go to Jesus to remove the abusive spirit from whoever has it in your family. Pray, believe and receive that which you request. Do not doubt or have unbelief when you stand praying. "Now I will not have you ignorant." Romans 1:13

Adults Too

Adults can be influenced also. Books, magazines, television, websites, people they surround themselves with, all can influence people. Subconsciously or consciously, people may want to become what they are fed from various media, which can be bad or good. If you are unsure what to read, watch on television, surf on the internet, people to hang around with, once again, go to Jesus. Make Him your best friend and He will never mislead you. Let Him direct your daily and nightly paths. People who obey God are not bored at all. They are entertained by things that won't corrupt them and hurt them or others now or later.

Have you noticed when your kids act differently it has a lot to do with if they have changed playmates, friends or behaving like someone they have seen on television? The words they use and/or their behavior becomes modified. Well, adults do it too. That is why it is important to feed ourselves with good material and surround ourselves with good people. -Birds of a feather flock together.

Plant positive seeds and expect a positive harvest. Positive thoughts of any kind are planted in your mind. Positive trees only produce positive fruits and negative trees only produce negative fruit. It is up to you to decide what you want planted or uprooted.

Negative People

Defiled people zero in on the negative in situations, whether it's in regular conversation, activities or whatever it is. They are not happy for other people's success. They try to destroy people's dreams and ideas of becoming successful or being happy. They complain without giving solutions. They aren't happy people, they are pessimists. Some people take compliments as insults. They find the negative in nearly everything and everyone. They walk around with a cloud of doom around them because they see things through a bad filter. It is because they are defiled. "…them that are defiled and unbelieving is nothing pure; but even their mind and conscience is defiled." -Titus 1:15. Pray for those people to become pure and perfect.

We will now proceed to another fruitful garden. I hope you have learned from this journey what we plant is what we will harvest and grow; what we grow is what we will sow positively or negatively.

Remember this quote by the great Theologian Reinhold Niebuhr wrote, "God, grant me the serenity to accept the things I can change; the courage to change the things I can change; and the wisdom to know the difference."

We give power to people and things that are so undeserving of us. Why give permission for someone to drain your spirits who does not have the ability or power to replenish it.

49

Prayer!

Father we come now in the name of Your Son, Jesus, thanking you Lord for another day you have granted unto us. We thank You Lord for Your many blessings, both big and small. Lord we come asking that you please remove any negative thought or deed away from us. We thank You for our friends, our families, our neighbors, being under Your grace, Lord. Make us all to obey You Lord; keeping Your commandments; doing the things You command us to do. I make my requests known to You and patiently await to receive them according to Your will, in Jesus name we pray. Amen!

Water and nourish your garden for a bountiful harvest. Let nothing weigh you down.

Surrender Everything Even Doubt.

Chapter IV

River of Readiness!

Where does the river flow?

Always moving and on the go.

It never stops. It never stands.

You must be ready to step off the land.

It's constantly drifting at a steady pace.

Are you ready to get in this race?

Step right up. Get in line, because

if you don't you will be left behind.

Please move fast and don't you wait,

Don't delay so you won't be too late.

As we cruise along the River of Readiness, fasten your life vest. It's time to explore the rivers of living water. In John 7:38, Jesus *said, "He that believeth on me, as the scripture hath said, out of the belly shall flow rivers of living water." "But sanctify the Lord God in your hearts: and be ready always to give an answer to every man that asketh you a reason of the hope that is in you with meekness and fear." 1 Peter 3:15 ...Be ready!*

We are living in a fast-paced world. Time waits on no man at all. Passing of time is consistent as is the flow of water. It's always moving. There is life in moving water. It's beneficial to all men. Water is a significant element in survival and resident to many living fish that nourishes us all.

Get in or Get Left

Today's way of living is very fast-paced with developments in technology that are important in nearly every facet of studying and daily living. There's the information super highway, the internet, texting, faxing, Instagram, emailing, face-chatting, you name it. Things are on our shelves in stores before they're introduced to the consumer. You either get in where you fit in, or get left behind. There's no mediator to say, "Stop. Let's give the consumers time to catch up with the new inventions in technology."

Technology has evolved but what about us? Do we know how to use todays resources to make life run smoother? Hosea 4:6, "My people are destroyed for lack of knowledge."

Always be ready. So many blessings have been missed because we weren't ready. Time matters greatly. One does not wait at home for the bus or plane departure. If you are not there in the terminal waiting, you will be left behind. Know your position learn it well and do right by it.

Receive

When we pray, make our request known to God, verbally. Believe we will receive them and prepare to receive, that which we have requested. If you are too busy worrying, stressing with your head glued to your text messaging, social networks, not paying attention and just engulfed in your own world, you may miss out on what you asked to receive. Don't ask someone to hand you something but your hands are closed to not receive it or you are looking elsewhere, like relay runners passing the baton, but one runner has his hand closed and misses receiving the baton. You lose every time no matter how far you are ahead. Take your focus off things of the world. "Finally, brethren, whatsoever things are true, whatsoever things are honest, whatsoever things are just, whatsoever things are pure, whatsoever things are lovely, whatsoever things are of good report; if there be any virtue, and if there be any praise, think on these things." Philippians 4:8v "If ye then be risen with Christ, seek those things which are above, where Christ sitteth on the right hand of God. Set your affection on things above, not on things on the earth." -Colossians 3:1-2.

Don't be addicted to your fancy devices, and technologies of the world. Everything we do, do it in moderation.

Local Broadcasting

If a meteorologist gives a forecast for bad weather, it's up to us to either prepare for it or not. Preparation is important to exercise. We're here on the earth preparing to live throughout eternity. Now, is for us to prepare. Also, being ready here on earth is an exercise for being ready for when Jesus returns.

We are given one book that instructs us on how to live. It is up to us to follow it to live forever. Some people only follow some of the instructions because they want to live the way they see fit, but wonder why certain things don't go the way they hoped it would. The bible is our blueprint for living a long, healthy, prosperous life here on the earth and in Heaven. It works just like in building a house. Use God's blueprint and the plain will be grand.

Be Ready!

I am on my way out of the door and my phone rings. I answer, "Hello?"

The voice on the other end replies, "Hey I need a favor. I received a call about getting a job, but I need a ride. Can you pick me up?"

I reply, "Sure, I was on my way out to make it across town in an hour. See you in a few minutes."

I pull up, toot my horn and I hear a voice say, "Wait! I have to do something first."

Fifteen minutes go by and they're still not ready. I can't wait any longer.

Later in the day, I am bombarded with angry responses to my leaving without the passenger in tow. It is somehow my fault. Never once did they mention the reason why they were left. -Get yourself together!

Hurricane Katrina

I was formerly from New Orleans until hurricane Katrina hit in August 2005. No one I knew was prepared for the extent of such an American catastrophe. Many lives were ruined or lost because of various reasons and unfortunate one being, lack of preparedness on every level.

My family and I were ready in a since because we had the means to get out of the horrific ordeal. We made it a point to have insurance, transportation and a little money that helped keep us afloat, but one thing we were not prepared for was the loss of so many lives and things. Hurricanes or emergencies could strike at any time. It can and has caused substantial losses but we must learn to be ready to get out harm's way. It's a time to prepare and a time to be ready. Not get ready!

Being Prepared

Saving money is one of the keys to being ready, in addition to many other factors. Suppose you receive a job opportunity, but you can't get there because you do not have transportation or bus fare to get there. Who's to blame? Don't blame others for your lack of being ill prepared. Be ready!

Education is another key in being prepared. Knowledge is one of the most powerful tools to obtain. Learning a trade or gaining a skill takes time, money and dedication. There are classes for nearly everything you can imagine. We need to invest more in ourselves than in stocks and nonsense things. Whatever you do or become remember that you are a person first before any title you can obtain.

No Compromising!

Do not give up when you are changing things in your life. Adversity will come about to try and deter you from changing for the better. The adversary (the devil) doesn't like you leaving him behind. Besides whom will he get to do his work? He will try holding on to you at all costs, but don't turn back to him because the second grip is stronger than the first if he gets you back. Have a plan and let nothing distract you from it. Stay strong because he's going to tug to see if you are weak in any way. After a while, he will see it's useless because of your strength, determination and protection from God. Notice I never once mention any of this would be easy however it will be well worth it.

You are either your weight (anchor) or your will. It is up to you to decide. Education strengthens abilities. Abilities help increase your income and income and a positive attitude can take you places.

Disguise

I was waiting on a blessing, waiting every day.

The mail man dropped by, I didn't let him inside.

I sent him on his way.

I am waiting for a blessing. I wish it would hurry up and come.

Then my phone rang loud.

I said, "I won't answer for a while because it will waste too much time talking on the line anyway.

I am waiting for my blessing."

Lord do you hear me now?

Was it a lie?

Then the Lord replied, "The mailman."

"The mailman?!" I cried, "But I didn't let him inside.

I whisked him off that day."

"Then I called and you didn't answer at all."

"I know."

"So, your blessing was postponed, need I say.

No, you weren't denied, and I surely don't lie.

I will send it another way." Just be ready always.

Blessings come in all forms and they can be delivered by any available body that God chooses.

On your Mark!

Pretend we're about to race, "Get on your mark! Get ready! Set…Go!"

What are you doing? Why didn't you go? What's stopping you? The race has begun and you have some catching up to do if you want to win you must begin.

Well, being a winner can also mean finish what you start. Don't quit. Oh, now, you've started moving, so let's move on. Don't forget; make time away from technology, or anything and anyone that hinders you from prayer, meditation and obeying God.

Go to God and ask Him what your calling is. Pray about it. Meditate. Talk with the elders of the church. Once you know what service you are to provide here on the earth, then start doing it. Don't delay. If you must go to school to learn it, enroll in school. If you must take lessons, get a teacher. You must know your position before you play your position. Whatever it is, start now. Just DO it! Again, I say, "Get on your mark! Get ready! Set…Go!" I know you are moving now.

Do know that you must be equipped for any position we have in this life. Yes, I mean from being a spouse to an Indian chief. You can't be given deadly weapons as being a policeman without the proper training so how do one expect to be a partner without learning the lesson of being single first. It is so important to learn you and being a whole person in sound body, spirit and mind before one can offer or render themselves to another. We are sometime to weak, selfish, inflexible, unstrapped and whatever else you can think of as a single person to know how to compromise in a relationship with another person. Some may say, My way or no way." When we hear that we should automatically go the other way. Make yourself a ready person but being ready doesn't mean that everything comes about is for you to experience.

Being ready and knowing yourself allows you to step up to the plate but doesn't have to swing at every ball pitched. That statement is major for many situations. You will learn to pick your poison in different affairs.

Huddle

Once in the huddle plays are called that are to be carried out by an individual team mates. A quarterback receives the ball from the center, he than looks for a receiver to throw the ball too if none is available he has the options of running to gain yardage himself, throw a rush pass that may cause an interception, or throw the ball to various players if the targeted wide- receiver isn't open. They may end up losing a play. Now think of this from a spiritual stand point. We pray receive divine directions from God and yet when it is time to receive what is to be given to us we are ill prepared because it sometimes requires our actions, not distractions or what we think is best for us. The answer to the prayer has been tossed up in the air but we stopped paying attention. We end up missing out. Be ready and available to receive all the time what is ours to receive.

Realize, Every Awakening Day is Yours

As this river tour ends and we are back on the shore let the river's current be with us forever more. It is bound to keep you moving so flow with the current. All dead creatures are pushed aside to allow the living water to keep that which is living alive. Be blessed and be ready.

Chapter V

The Congo of Confrontation!

This was one on of the hardest chapters to write. We sometimes tend to blame our setbacks or hang-ups on other people, but sometimes, as we have discussed in previous chapters, often time it is ourselves who need adjusting. Yes, other people can cause us to stumble but don't allow it to ever let you fall. Work on you. Like Iyanla Vanzant, would say, "On It."

Will You Listen

I stepped right up, cleared my throat and stared deeply into her eyes, while trying to remember the words I had rehearsed to tell her. Then the words began to pour from my lips. "You have smiled and laughed when I know you were hurting but I don't think you ever understood your worth. When I tried loving you, you pushed me away. You were still bitter about wrong choices you made in the past."

She stared back at me, as I watched a tear roll slowly down her face; not a smile in her lips without a whisper at all. Not wanting to see this but I stood bold and tall. I said, "If it wasn't for you, I could be a better person you see. You tug and pull as stubborn as you can be. I sat and watched how you broke the rules. Then for your defense you built, walls to never feel hurt again. Not letting anyone in, no one at all. I wanted to be a good daughter, sister, a friend and saint most of all. You said not so, because others would mistreat you when you show love or that you care. So further inward I go," but I said this has to stop! "I don't want you to oversee me anymore. I am sorry I guess I must let you go. I thought it would be so easy getting you off my back. You're just like the adversary always trying to attack. When I say, I am done I am done for good. I allow you to do things that no one else could. Like fornicating, lying and cheating in sin. You know not to play with the devil. He is not your friend. I am all grown up now and I have prayed you away, only for you to come again another day."

I said, "Trina, marry your faith and be ready when called. Positive energy doesn't deflate. I forgive you truly for hurting yourself. Now stand up bold and receive your wealth."

As I began to walk away I saw a new reflection of myself in the mirror that day. Mirrors don't lie. I simply walked away. I died to myself and had a total transformation need I say. You cannot fill a void with everyone and everything you would only be hurting yourself repeatedly. Cry out unto the Lord Jesus Christ your King. He has the power to heal you, mold you and console you from everything. If only you have the faith and believe you shall receive.

I could have very well blamed my actions on what I lack in life as a child, or give excuse as to why I accepted a dysfunctional relationship but I focus solely on me and what needed to be done to address self and forgetting all else. No, I am not perfect by no means but I getting better every day.

Check

We must learn to confront the things in our lives that we know are not in right standings. We do routine maintenance on cars, computers, machinery, but rarely on ourselves. This could be a reason why that when we see a Dr. we get such bad news. It took forever to get check on by a Doctor. You know that unfamiliar mole that has now grown into a malignant tumor art not be.

We are our best critic and it is to only make us better and stronger. You can discover new self- respect when you put your perspectives in check. We may need to have a complete over haul. If you cannot stand in the mirror toe to toe with self how can you stand up to anyone else, if you're not true to you? No, you can fake this until you make it. You are untrue to self and that is acceptable but when others are untrue to you their damn to hell. Learn to be genuine through and through and your mirrored image will be that to you. What we are as a person sometimes that mate gravitates to our inner being.

So, with while saying that obtain help to become clean to the core of self. Seek the word of God which is the only thing that can pierce through the spirit and soul of man. He can cleanse you thoroughly. Remember if you can't check yourselves please don't check anyone else.

Who's Responsible?

How a person was reared affects their life if they let it, but in a court of law, don't depend on a judge to take that into consideration when making his judgment. You are the responsible party. Your soul will be on trial before going to your eternal destination and no one else's. Do as God tell us to do now and let Jesus take the pain of your past away from you today so we can live freely.

Lots of wisdom can be found in the book of Proverbs, but knowledge comes from seeking and applying the word of God.

Confrontations do not have to be negative therefore it should not be frown upon when you confront people, including yourself. I am not saying your past should not affect you and to just get over it. There are all forms of counseling and you should seek help for whatever is keeping you in bondage. You can be freed and yes even your burden can be lifted. Trust God and believe that you can be healed and become whole again. Only puzzles should come in pieces not people minds or their spirits.

Yes, there are such things as mind disorders. Such as Bipolar, Anxiety, Major depressions, PTSD and so forth, but there is also help. Seek it for the betterment of you.1-888-611-3284 or! -800-273-8255 press 1.

Self-Searching

Some people react to pain from the past in forms of self-destruction/ self-hate. When a void exists in our-selves, it is best dealt with going to God to fill it. We all want to feel accepted and love, but though we have emotions and feelings, we must never allow things or people to tear us down. If it or they do not have the power or ability to build us up. Don't allow them to tear us down. This just like having a security monitor but not security themselves. The monitor still must report to security. So, go to the one that could build you that has the power and capabilities to do it all. Replenish, repair, rejuvenate and can rebuke the devour for our sake. Where would we be if Jesus emotions had gotten in the way of HIM dyeing on the cross for us all. We must understand that sometime it is pure love to give away what and who we love for the good of the matter. We are all here for a purpose and if you don't know what that purpose is, then ask the Spirit of God. Become born again of God to where your conscience want allow you to sin. Go to Jesus to be cleansed with His blood, because nothing can penetrate the blood of Jesus. Know your calling and do it. The devil doesn't like being rebuked in the name of Jesus, so speak, "I am protected by the blood of Jesus and nothing can penetrate it. You are a liar Satan and you are rebuked from tampering with me or the people I love.

Go and be cast into the sea in the name of Jesus!" This is our protection. Use it.

Cleaning Starts at Home First

Take some time to get to know your -self. Really sit down with the television, radio, computer devices all off. Ask the Spirit of God to show you clearly what it is you should be doing every day, every second of your life. How can you effectively help others if you're all messed up? How can you help others in need if you can't even help yourself? I know you just thought I am not trying to help anyone. What affect from your bondage you are leaving with your children, your love ones and or your significant others? Let Jesus cleanse you and make you into a whole new person.

Take a moment to clear up thoughts to jot down things that need confronting in your life with you, before you branch out to others. Let's make ourselves a whole person first before we render ourselves to others. We don't buy broken products at the store, less not offer a broken spirit to no-one and don't receive damage goods. You would end up paying a much bigger price for damage goods. This may seem a little cynical but it is easier to walk away from a situation when you are complete and no one or nothing you need from others to complete you. We all have issues and only taxes are exempt here. You are independent not a dependent. No one else can carry you, but you. Forgive yourself and others and move on. You can do it, and if you do it with Christ, you can do it a lot easier. For the one that just thought but you don't know the things that I have done or the people that I have hurt. Ask for forgiveness in all sincerity and God will forgive you too. Although you will be rewarded diligently and you will still be forgiven and that frees the spirit to make you whole again. God still loves you. Thanks for turning from your wicket ways it will do you good. Learn to love yourself again and others will do the same.

While touring through the Congo I hope you could see the beautiful parrots and exotic birds in the trees and not just the trees itself (just your problem). Don't allow the thickness of your outer core hinder the goodness inside of you. Sometimes we may have to look deeper than what we initially see. Hence the saying, "Can't see the forest for the trees." Pearls are beautiful in the inside of the dirtiest, hardest oyster shell. No one will know of its beauty until you truly open the shell up.

Although everyone is predestinated, we still have free will just use it to make Godly choices.

Forgiving

Forgiving others and yourself makes room for love. We can go further in life with a pure heart with no shackles around our ankles or neck. When we forgive, we physically feel a load being lifted off us. Hatred and not forgiving hinders us. It harms self. When you truly forgive someone, this should not be the topic at every dinner table, family functions or gatherings. Let it go. Forgiving in your heart will keep it off your mind. Don't try to get revenge because remember whatever we plant, that is what will grow. So, if you try to do wrong to someone because they did wrong, it just comes back to wrong being done to you, perhaps by someone different or situation may not be in your favor. Plant love and receive love. Keep the commandments of God, that way you can't go wrong.

Exposed

Yes, my own woes were put in front of me,

So, they could no longer taunt me.

Exposure of hurts, uncovering the mask,

self-endangerment will no longer rekindle or rehash.

I've called you out into the light, darkness can't hide you anymore.

You've been evicted I'm taking my keys and locking my spiritual door.

I have forgiven myself and this is the end.

You have been exposed pain and fear never will I allow you to come up again.

This time I win.

The Congo's journey has come to an end.

Take forgiveness with you and above all love. Go to Jesus and let Him cleanse you of all sin.

My analogy of con-front-ation,

Con means contra or against.

-front is the part or side of anything that faces forward.

-ation is abstract to change a noun to a verb, which I love because it shows action. This part of the word allows us at free will to change things around or for some to spruce things up. Remember a verb is an action word. Faith without action is dead. (James 2:14 KJV) We must do something.

Can you put your issues which are the action, place them in front of you and come against what you need to change or what has held you back? even if it is self. Remember from the previous chapter Rivers of living water is in our belly.

Chapter VI

Liberty in Letting Go!

I remember when I was in school studying to become a practical nurse. Psychology was my favorite subject. I learned that we are all two letters from being in-sane. I laugh sometimes because I could have identified with all the behaviors at one time or another. I just found that the behaviors and the functioning of the mind are awesome. By the end of this chapter, I hope that you have a better insight on how holding on and letting go is processed by the mind.

What's your Twenty?

We will first visit the stages of grief. I read a book entitled, <u>Death and Dying</u> by Elisabeth Kubler-Ross years past. It was given to me by a co-worker when my mom was terminally ill. (Patricia Doughty) I also studied her method in school called, "The Stages of Grief," which were listed and discussed to be five stages of grief at that time:

Stage 1 - "Denial:"

"The mind's first defense is to deny what it is not familiar with." When news of losing someone close, receiving bad test results, losing a job or etcetera is given, some will accept the news immediately while others may deny it. Different people tend to process and or accept major events differently.

People are in our lives for a reason and for different durations. We form bonds with some while they are here. After they have served their purpose, we don't want to let them go.

Everybody knows death is inevitable and most are afraid because it is unknown and we don't want to leave those we are close to on the earth. Some people I stated earlier, are afraid to let go of what is familiar and make other people or things become their crutch. Some choose to deny that they are losing someone or something dear to them. They may deny the loss for days, months or years. They may feel out of sync, not on the same accord with things in their lives because they are still holding on to what is no longer there and what is familiar to them.

Stage 2 "Anger:"

"Anger may be felt because some feel powerless and desperately want to save the person or thing that is in the process of being lost, or they do not want to feel the pain of losing someone or something dear to them." Some may become envious of others who aren't experiencing tremendous sadness and may express their anguish by lashing out or keeping the anger in, becoming increasingly bitter.

Stage 3" Bargaining:"

We hear people say, "I will go to church more or study longer," or whatever the bargain is, "If I can have it or keep it." It may help to think of the prospective loss or actual loss as you're holding a lit candle in the sun. You must let it go. Get counseling if you to aid you in letting go or find it difficult in doing so. There is no need to go at this along.

Bargaining is a familiar activity. For instance, we increase our hours at work if we can't afford something we want. We make a way for the things we want or want to keep. We negotiate if it's an option, or even do a trade. Do whatever it may take. Some try bargaining to keep their loved-one or thing that they don't want to lose.

Stage 4 "Depression:"

"The act of disconnecting from life, love, job, friends and etcetera." This person is weighed down with burdens because they do not want to let go. Physically and emotionally stressed and saddened.

Grieving is not a death sentence it is a process to go through in any loss that is dear to us. Don't lag and drag burdens along. It's like diving in a pool with weights around your ankles. How long can one stay afloat? Do what needs to be done to rid your-self of these heavy burdens and not just drain the pool.

If you or others find yourself in a long state of depression or have suicidal thoughts, seek professional help immediately. Call on Jesus, especially.

Stage 5 "Acceptance:"

We must know that everything or everybody we let go is not a loss. We can gain so much by letting go. I said earlier in another chapter how can one receive with closed hands. How can one conceive with a closed mind? Let you mind know what is wanted or unwanted so when something unacceptable comes about our defense mechanism will kick in.

I know for me in most of my dealings, I must rehearse in my mind and exercise my rights before any action will follow.

No one complete a successful diet just by waking up one morning and doing it. It was excepted and rehearsed in the mind first. Yes, things are done cold turkey but for most of us it's prepared in the mind first. Do you know of any one that was together for years and just ended up at attorney's office partitioning divorce? No one said any of this would be easy but don't compromise. Set your standards. Know what you want and what you are willing to except or let go. Stop being so afraid of being by yourself. Notice I didn't say being alone because a person that is alone is not always lonely.

Write it down. Do a check list, and stick with it. You can be the best worker, spouse, friend or what have you.

Remember, accept the things we cannot change.

Tomatoes

You and two others or given tomato seeds to plant at the same time. One planter was always fascinated by the growing of tomatoes, so she immediately planted the seeds. Her neighbors often commented on how beautiful her tomatoes would grow, which made her happy. The other planted expeditiously as well, watering and nurturing her seeds. Her harvest was a blessing to her and others also.

You on the other hand, became envious of the others because of the positive accolades they received about the richness and how beautiful their gardens grew. You decided not to plant because you like the way the seeds look, so you kept them packaged. Next, you find out the first sower's return, made her extra money because the home magazine wanted to have her garden featured in their magazine, while the other planter harvested enough to sell at the local market. Her seeds produced more than just the tomatoes themselves.

Now, your seed profited you nothing because you never took them out the package. You settled for the seeds and became most familiar with them instead of letting them go because you became too attached. This aggravated you because they were no benefit to you later.

The moral of this story is, the seeds had to be let go to get their full benefit of being beauty in the garden and the fullness your gain as a tasty, profitable treat. Keeping the seeds instead of harvesting them as an abundance of fruit is not the intent for them. They should have been planted, nurtured and water.

You can't keep a baby a baby forever, or a child and child forever just to console you. Not fair to the child. Train them up in the way they should as the Bible states and when they get older they want part from it. Stop hindering the growth of others as well.

You're holding yourself back when you try to hold something that is not for you to hold anymore. Don't keep yourself in bondage, trying to keep others or something else in bondage that needs to be let go.

Know when to let go. Stop giving oxygen to a dead situation. We hold on to a piece of a mate, a terrible job, past baggage or that ragged old car because of their sentimental value or convenience not for their capabilities or purpose. A piece of something to you could be a whole something to someone else or something else. Don't be puzzled. Let what is not yours go free; release it; free to live out its intent, and grant others their growth with or without you. Being selfish can also cause a setup for a setback with self.

What Is Welcomed?

The mind is where we welcome welfare or warfare. We choose. Go through the process if that's what it takes to become a healthier you. There is a major difference in letting go and giving up.

Here's a point to ponder: People sometimes find it hard to let go in relationships or friendships because of their lack and insecurities in themselves; not so much of how they really feel about you. They try to keep you in that place to keep them comfortable; using you as their crutch. This stunts your growth and disrupts your journey. Sometimes we may have to tour de France alone yet not be lonely. Your journey is for better living, just less the baggage.

Letting Go!

Letting go is not always easy.

I find it rather hard.

Although I need to change some things in my life,

I will keep my trust in GOD.

No I am not giving up.

I am simply moving on.

To ward off heavy burdens I 've been holding on for much too long.

It's not what you have, but what you are willing to let go.

Letting go is not about losing love, your heart or emotional detachment.

It is what's embedded in the mind.

Your mind can change. It's just a simple matter of time.

It's not always about a person it could be a place or thing,

It's amazing how we evolve and grow,

when we are willing to let go of our emotions, people, places or things.

To not let go, can cause people to not get along in relationships, companies, social gatherings, on jobs, you name it. Go to God to know when and how to let go. Perhaps, it's only for you to have dinner or a movie with someone, not to try and get into a committed relationship, marriage or partnership in business. You're going against the grain when ignoring the signs indicating, "Get over it. Let...IT...GO!" Don't tug with the war at hand. Let go and let God. It's not a lost but a gain. The fight is tougher swimmer against the current. There is liberty in letting go it can help you grow. You must be willing, determined and unafraid to let go of burdens, people or things.

Sometime one must let go of a tight grip to be save. You will still be worthy, loved and so forth. It is mature of you to know and can let go what is not for you to have. Your gut feelings are tired of being ignored. Trust it sometimes and learn what good it could do you. Your life will flow better. It doesn't mean that other people or not good people their just not right for you. It doesn't mean because you have on a size 10 that is what fits you. You know how relieved you become once you get home and take something off that is ill fitting. Just think of something that you have worn whether it be a garment, shoe, hat, ring or what comes to mind. Remember the relief you felt once it was no longer there. Yes, for some of us we needed to gain our normal feeling back in that area or just be delighted from the simple relief. Once you let go of what have been holding you back, once you let go of what you allowed to keep you in bondage you will see wasted time and tears. You may need to grieve it a moment or on the other hand the relief may be so gratifying you have no time for grief. Thankfulness for the weight that has been lifted. Can't you feel the smile coming about you. You should feel lighter. Just smile. Now that a change has come. Be wise in your choosing.

Remember life on earth is a gift that eventually has an expiration date. When will you open it up? It's counting down. Let go and let God.

Chapter VII

Paradise of Prosperity

"And JESUS said unto him, Verily I say unto thee, today thou shalt be with me in paradise," Luke 23:43. Paradise is a "pleasure ground" or "park" or "a king's Garden;" a world of happiness and rest hereafter as per Dic.com

What is Your Paradise?

What makes you happy? What relaxes or calms you? For some it may be a simple break from the kids, from house cleaning, taking a vacation, bubble bath, a good church service, winning the lottery, watching a good movie, time alone with someone special, helping others, a day off from work or just reading a good book. Everybody's paradise is unique for themselves. Whatever your paradise is, you can have it. It is up to us to live in paradise daily. It is not always that a circumstance should change but it may be the way you look at the circumstance. Another angle can project a contrasting view. The view of a triangle if held straight would look like one point with two side-views, but if you look at the same triangle upside down there would be two side views with one point. Ha! Get my point, still a triangle, similarly to the circumstance. Try a more diverse approach at dealing with it. Step back. Get a different view. It's hard to see your situation when you're in it. Notice most people has said, when I look back at the things I have done or been through. So, take a break, step back and look at you in action to even know if it lines up with your paradise.

Stop crying about what life has dealt you. Go to Jesus to lay you cares on him, in the meantime when life gives you lemons make lemonade. Now, if life gives you apples, bake a pie. Complaining about your circumstance will not aid you in the garden of paradise; it is not even welcomed.

Do correlate paradise with peace not chaos and calamity. Learn to build the walls of serenity in your mind. Everyone should have a place to go to escape from the day to day of life. Remember the introduction spoke on how the foundation should be solid and the blueprint is your design depending upon your faith. Just how life is. If it's a one chance shot. We should give all we got.

Not permitted

Don't permit unwanted spiritual guests, negativity, anger, hurts or pains. This is the key for advancements in a paradise.

Keep your angels at you gates of your mind daily to filter anything and anyone that's not permitted. Computers have spy ware and we can have spiritual spy ware. Be wise, strong, determine and be committed. It is up to you to build character, high self- esteem and so forth. Have dignity about yourself. A no-body would not just step up to your paradise that has functionality and all together. Broken people look for broken things that they think they can fix. Complexity is a foreign object to some and not easily cable of reaching and it takes much to pair up. However nearly anyone can handle simplicity therefore don't be simple for nothing or no one. Be the jewelry that is lock away in the case and it needs security and keys to examine it. You are the only one who can allow entry to your paradise. It has a key that only you hold. You can then have control of whom and what is there. So be careful of entrance access and denial.

You may or may not have keys to open or close anything tangible. Do know you have the keys to your own paradise. You have the right to evict anyone or anything that's not welcome.

If your paradise is being interrupted via the phone line politely say I am hanging up now. If in person politely say. I am excusing myself now. walk away or excuse them from your presence. We do not have to accept what others so eagerly wants to give us. Life teaches, people tend to hold on to valuables. When some are willing to give something away so freely check its value. It's probably not worth much or nothing at all. Give your best and expect nothing less.

Noah built the Ark for him and his family and animals 2 by 2.

He didn't allow anyone that talks negatively about the ship size color or how many rooms affect the building of what saved them. It should not have matter anyway because of him and the works of God he did save his family. Just think if he was so emotional and allow his feelings of what others had to say about him building a ship on dry land.

We must realize there are people that would rip you to shreds if you allow them. What if he had ignored God words to him and listen to the nay saying that wasn't even chosen for the vessel. They would have one thinking that the blessing they have is a burden. We must be just as bold as they are but in decency and in order. People will learn your character or your new character. Build an heir about you. Listen to God's word.

Let's take Noah name and mix up the letters a bit. Let's go from Noah to NAOH. When someone steps in your realm that's not wanted think of Noah and the Ark but use this acronym. NAOH: Not Approved Over Here. No matter what it is you are the driver of your life. Zap negativity and strife out with NAOH. Make sticky notes to remind you what once was isn't any more.

You know I like scenario's let's do a few here.

Your sitting home studying for a major test in the A.M. and the phone rings. On the other end, you hear its Timeless Thursday at 'The Not for long Club" come on we should go, I am studying you say, you're always studying they reply it's not that important. Think of NAOH. And Zap it. Not Approved Over Here! And say bye bye, bye. Yes! You did it. It may not be easy the first round but it will become more and more easy when you realize your closer to your goals or when your more at peace.

Scenario 2:

Sitting inside you and your family. Cooking watching T.V. There is a knock at the door. You look out, it's one of your single home boys. Hey lets go for a ride man I'm bored. Well I'm cooking now and hanging with the fam. That's all you seem to do lately. Yeah right. Let's go for a ride bruh we want be long. We can get a smoke in take the edge off. You're then thinking yeah, your right, this week was a little long as your thoughts begin to sway. Just as you are about to turn your pots off your baby say daddy I am hungry. It snatches you back. Think of Noah, ZAP it out of your house. Not Approved Over Here. They are about to pull you into a mess. Family would have had to wait until whenever and everything would have been out of sync. Remember your friend is single.

I want even start on conversations from your mother, father, spouses or someone that you are close too. Even more, ones you look up too. We must remember they come in negative sizes as well. So, handle accordingly.

Scenario 3:

You know the sky is blue on a pretty summer day. You know you love summer and picnics and so forth. You have gotten your watermelon, blanket, a nice book and ready to enjoy this beautiful day. Your neighbor sees you as you are leaving out. Where to she says. Your excitement overflowing and you blurt out a picnic in the park. Oh girl, the sun is too hot. You will be sweating. Do you have your mosquito repellant because this time of year they are bad and I know Zika supposed to be close to our city? Since the baby with you watch where you put the blanket cause them ants are a mess.

My smile has now subsided. Do you see why it has diminish? The oxygen had been snatch out of my joy.

So is she a keeper or does she need NAOH, zap out of my paradise.

Just negative all the time. Be joyous!

Something that I always thought was a little confusing. When someone wants to remind you of something, they would say, don't forget to do x,y z. Replace don't forget with remember to do x,y z. That is better for memory. Once you hear don't forget most times it's already forgotten. That was just a thought to share with you while thinking about negative things.

Staying the Course

The tourist attractions visited in this journey, all are related in obtaining and managing better living. The navigation can be preprogrammed, but it's up to us to stay the course. Our paradise is what we make it and how long we tend to reside there is up to us. Everybody or everything should not be welcomed to our paradise. It's for you to enjoy the beauty of living, sharing, loving and giving. It's up to you to hold on or let go of the wheel of your life that you are driving.

Think of the serenity, picture that special beautiful place that keeps you taking another breath and placing a smile in your heart. Embrace it always whenever you wish to it is yours for the asking.

Prosper

"Beloved I wish above all things that thou mayest prosper and be in health, even as thy soul prospereth." - III John 1-2.

Some may dwell in good health and live for many years, but their souls may be vexed. Prosperity is individualized by its own maker, so let God put His Spirit in our body.

What you would like to prosper in? It is your will, your desire. Every blessing is stemmed from your actions or deeds. Psalm 37:4, "Delight yourself also in the Lord, and He shall give you the desires of your heart." Thus, one must not live ungodly and expect Godly rewards. If you sow Godly seeds in tithes and offering He will rebuke the devourer for our sakes, (Malachi 3:11).

"And these are they which are sown on good ground; such as hear the word, and receive it, and bring forth fruit, some thirty-fold, some sixty, and some a hundred. "-Mark 4:20 Take the lady in the previous chapter, who understood she needed to sow, water and nurture the seeds for them to return to her more than what was sown. This is one of the ways to prosper and be in good health. Holding on and carrying burdens causes stress which can elevate your blood pressure, which in turn could damage your kidneys that then affects the heart and/or etcetera. GOD does not want us sick.

 He wants us in divine health with a sound mind. He placed everything we need in the earth to nourish and heal us.

What good is it to be rich and prosperous but have bad health? You would not be able to enjoy the prosperity. That's a burden, not a blessing. We must take care of our bodies. Fasting is another form of cleansing the body from all impurities/toxins. High blood pressure, cancer, diabetes, depression, multiple sclerosis, gout, arthritis, heart disease, obesity, sickle cell, aids and all sicknesses and diseases, be thou removed and be cast into the sea in the name Jesus! Sin destroys the body, so get rid of it.

There is literature for every disease known to man in books, the internet, from doctor 's, etcetera. We are meant to be a prosperous people. It's up to us to live in the Paradise of Prosperity. If you don't take care of you, then who will? Everyone has their own measure of what success and prosperity is, therefore don't judge. We all choose our paradise.

Paradise

Walk into your secret door,

where the devil can't trample your floor,

isolating it from every man.

Avoid distractions and take a stand.

My paradise is what I so desire.

Igniting the flame and keeping the fire.

Renouncing Satan and excepting Jesus in my heart.

Never again shall we depart.

My paradise is what I make it not allowing anyone to forsake it.

Partake in your pleasure and remember it is your treasure.

My paradise is

_____

_____

_____

I will

_____

_____

_____ too make sure I dwell in paradise daily; my heavenly place on earth.

Pleasure Awaits, Relaxing Atmosphere Devine Indulgence Serenity Excels

I hope you have enjoyed your journey to better living and now it is up to you to live better. We discussed the tools needed for better living, now use them. Let nothing or no one hold you back. Keep positive energy, faith that won't fail, motivation the won't kill, be ready when called, confrontation that can heal, know when to let go, believe and be like Jesus and keep all of God's commandments. Continue in paradise forever more. This journey is nearing the end, but let yours continue. Learn to live again. Carrying extra baggage can harm you so leave it at the terminal. Go on with your life just less the baggage and strife. God, bless you and much love.

Until you read again.

Saints Needed

We are looking for a few good men and gender is not a factor here.

*We are not the Army but we pray more by 7 a.m. than most people do all day.

* We are not the Navy but we have rivers of living waters.

*We are not the Marines but "we wrestle not against flesh and blood, but against principalities, against powers, against the rulers of the darkness of this world, against spiritual wickedness in high places." -Ephesians 6:10.

Qualification:

Back sliders, gamblers, whore-mongers, fornicators, adulterers, liars, back-stabbers, murderers, drug dealers, prostitutes, molesters, homosexuals, thieves, false prophets, idolaters; all sinners

Experience:

Benefits:

Everlasting life, royal priesthood, to be king of kings, your name in the Book of Life

Salary:

Top pay upon tithing, "Open the windows of heaven, and pour you out a blessing, that you may not have room enough to receive it. "-Malachi 3:10.

"Give, and it shall be given unto you; good measure, pressed down, and shaken together, and running over, shall men give into your bosom. For with the same measure that ye meet with it shall be measured to you again." -Luke 6:38.

Equipment Needed:

The whole armor of God -the breast plate of righteousness, your feet shod with the preparation of truth, the gospel of peace, the shield of faith, the helmet of salvation and the sword of the Spirit, God 's word.

Don't wait to late, sign up today, this minute. This is recession proof.

Apply now:

"Confess with thy mouth the Lord Jesus and believe in thine heart that God hath raised Him from the dead, thou shalt be saved." -Romans 10:9 (Rebuke the devil in the name Jesus.)

Date of acceptance: _____

or renewed Date: _____

The angels in Heaven is rejoicing.

Prayer

Dear, Heavenly Father in Jesus name, thank You for the tourists who journey with me. Lord I ask that you give them strength where they are weak. Meet them at their needs. Let this motivational venture be a life changing experience for all who reads it. Fill any void, remove any hurt guilt or shame in Jesus name we pray. Let them know that they can leave their baggage with you to allow them to have less the burdens, allowing every one of them to travel further in their endeavors. Thank you for allowing them to journey with me and until we meet again. Amen.

Songs of the Heart

You are What Is Right

You are my flame in the darkest night.

You give me hope until the morning light.

So, I give to thee my deepest plight,

Because you are to me what is right.

You are to me what is right, you are to me what is right

You are to me what is right, you are what is truly right.

So, I sing praises of pure delight because you are to me what is right.

You are my Savior and you are my Friend.

You said you would be there until the end.

You gave me courage when I was afraid, you gave me new direction when I was misled.

You are to me what is right. You are to me what is right.

You are to me what is right. You are to me what is truly right.

Lord you never judge me when I was in sin. You only chastise me and you took me on in.

God, you kept me in my sound mine when I was confused, and you held me when I was used and abused.

You are to me what is right. You are to me what is right.

You are to me what is right. You are what is truly right.

Broken Shackles

He has broken the shackles and the chains.

So, I thank you Lord for another chance.

I have been redeemed and set free.

Thank you Lord for saving me.

He has kept my mind even when I had doubt.

His Grace and Mercy has bought me out.

I have been redeemed and set free.

I thank you Lord for the vic-to-ry.

He has broken the shackles and the chains.

I thank you Lord for a new-found dance.

I am lifting holy hands to give you praise, in Jesus name.

Yes, I am no longer bound no problems or nobody could keep me down.

It is my freedom I proclaimed. I am going to praise you Lord and I am not a shame.

He has broken the shackles and the chains.

Yes, we are no longer bound. No problems or nobody could keep us down.

We are redeemed and set free. So, thank you Lord for our vic-to-ry.

He has broken the shackles and the chains

Poem

Love

Love is beautiful and it should not hurt.

Some say love is give and take.

Love is an action word, but it starts in the mind.

Nurturer, water and delivered to the heart.

Love should not break you down or tear you apart.

Love is plentiful and should be shared.

Yes, there are many people that still care.

Love, love, love and this is my prayer.

About the author:

Trina Robertson, Christian, wife and mother of two wonderful children, Grandmother, Poet, Licensed Practical Nurse, and motivator. A native of New Orleans, Louisiana, currently resides in Baton Rouge. Louisiana. Motivating others is her passion. She loves writing, inspiring and uplifting others through her writing, fashion sense and speeches. She is also a motivational speaker for all occasions. C.E.O. of Motivating-U - Productions.

Reference:

Scriptures quoted are from the King James Version or NIV of the Bible.

"Just DO it" is the slogan of the brand name, NIKE as seen on television commercial.

Lyrics are from CD of Artist, Monica.

Stages of grief from Nursing psychology 2007/2008

All poetry and slogans is written by the author and can be purchase separately. Orders of any poetry, slogan, chants or songs can be purchase on T-shirts, totes, hats or mugs.